Growing Readers

Fathers

by Lola M. Schaefer

Consulting Editor: Gail Saunders-Smith, Ph.D.

Consultant: Phyllis Edelbrock, First-Grade Teacher,
University Place School District, Washington

Pebble Books

an imprint of Capstone Press
Mankato, Minnesota

1

Pebble Books are published by Capstone Press
818 North Willow Street, Mankato, Minnesota 56001
http://www.capstone-press.com

Library of Congress Cataloging-in-Publication Data
Schaefer, Lola M., 1950–
    Fathers/by Lola M. Schaefer
    p. cm—(Families)
    Includes bibliographical references and index.
    Summary: Simple text and photographs depict fathers and what they do with
their children.
    ISBN 0-7368-0256-8
    1. Fathers—Juvenile literature. 2. Father and child—Juvenile literature.
[1. Fathers. 2. Father and child.] I. Title. II. Series: Schaefer, Lola M., 1950–   Families.
HQ756.S32 1999
306.874'2—dc21   98-46119
                                                                                    CIP
                                                                                    AC

Note to Parents and Teachers

The Families series supports national social studies standards for units related to identifying family members and their roles in the family. This book describes and illustrates fathers and activities they do with their children. The photographs support emergent readers in understanding the text. The repetition of words and phrases helps emergent readers learn new words. This book also introduces emergent readers to subject-specific vocabulary words, which are defined in the Words to Know section. Emergent readers may need assistance to read some words and to use the Table of Contents, Words to Know, Read More, Internet Sites, and Index/Word List sections of the book.

Table of Contents

4

A father is a male parent.

Fathers make cookies.

Fathers go to the doctor.

Fathers read.

Fathers shop.

14

Fathers swim.

Fathers draw.

Fathers play.

Fathers hug.

Words to Know

cookie—a sweet, usually round and flat snack made from dough

doctor—someone trained to treat sick or injured people

draw—to make a picture

male—a boy or man; fathers are males.

parent—a person who produces young; fathers and mothers are parents.

read—to look at written or printed words and understand what they mean

shop—to go to stores to buy food and other items

Read More

Maccarone, Grace. *I Shop with My Daddy.* Hello Reader! New York: Scholastic, 1998.

Morris, Ann. *The Daddy Book.* World's Family Series. Parsippany, N.J.: Silver Press, 1996.

Rotner, Shelley, and Sheila M. Kelly. *Lots of Dads.* New York: Dial Books for Young Readers, 1997.

Saunders-Smith, Gail. *Parents.* People. Mankato, Minn.: Pebble Books, 1997.

Internet Sites

Father's Day
http://www.kidsdomain.com/holiday/dad

Fathers Day Page
http://www.delphi.com/care/preschool/
fathers_day_page.html

Happy Father's Day!
http://www.vbe.com/~gns/fathersday.html

Index/Word List

cookies, 7
doctor, 9
draw, 17
father, 5, 7, 9, 11, 13,
  15, 17, 19, 21
go, 9
hug, 21

make, 7
male, 5
parent, 5
play, 19
read, 11
shop, 13
swim, 15

Word Count: 26
Early-Intervention Level: 5

Editorial Credits
Mari C. Schuh, editor; Steve Weil/Tandem Design, cover designer and illustrator;
  Kimberly Danger and Sheri Gosewisch, photo researchers

Photo Credits
International Stock/ Earl Kogler, cover; Scott Barrow, 16
Ken Chernus/FPG International LLC, 12
PhotoBank, Inc./Bill Lai, 10
Photo Network/Myrleen Ferguson Cate, 6
Unicorn Stock Photos/MacDonald Photography, 20
Uniphoto, 4; Uniphoto/Michael A. Keller, 8
Visuals Unlimited/Peter Holden, 1; Jeff Greenberg, 14; Mark E. Gibson, 18

Special thanks to Joy Allison, Lori Hollenback, and Penny McCarthy, first-grade
teachers at Evergreen Primary in University Place, Washington, for reviewing books
in the Families series.